A Little Indulgence

CHOCOLATE

C H O C O L A T E

Printed in the United States of America
by G&R Publishing Co.

Distributed By:

Products

507 Industrial Street
Waverly, IA 50677

ISBN-13: 978-1-56383-230-7
ISBN-10: 1-56383-230-5
Item #6205

You have to admit, there is just something special about chocolate. There is something about this sweet treat that sets it apart from everything else consumable. Chocolate stands in a category of its own, but does not think too highly of itself to enhance a dessert or lend a helping hand to a lonely piece of fruit. Chocolate is rich and dark, light and sweet, hot and cold – almost as if to conquer any palate that falls under its pleasant spell. Chocolate is, let's face it, one of life's best indulgences.

In the shaded canopy of the thriving rainforests of Brazil, Indonesia or the Ivory Coast, chocolate emerges from the melon yellow pods of the cacao tree as a lonely seed – the cocoa bean. These beans hold the secret to a flavor that entices millions almost to the point of addiction, the flavor that fills dessert carts worldwide, the flavor that is synonymous with love – the flavor of chocolate.

To begin its journey, these special beans are removed from the hand-picked pods and left to harden, darken and develop the rich cocoa flavor held within. From this fermentation stage, the beans are transported to chocolate factories around the globe to be cleaned and stored.

The beans are then slowly spun in large, high-temperature roasters before a hulling machine separates the shell from the "nib" held inside. The nibs are then sent through milling, where they are ground into chocolate liquor – a smooth, dark stream of pure liquid chocolate.

Most chocolate liquor is then combined with the main ingredients of cocoa butter, sugar and milk before being molded into many shapes and variations.

So whip up a hot cocoa and take a moment to appreciate the immensely enjoyable flavor that first surfaces as a little seed. A world of chocolaty goodness lies ahead…

PERFECTLY CHOCOLATE
HOT COCOA
Makes 4 servings

8 tsp. hot cocoa mix,
  divided
Pinch of salt, divided

8 T. sugar, divided
4 C. milk, divided
1 tsp. vanilla, divided

In each of four coffee mugs, place 2 teaspoons hot cocoa mix, a pinch of salt and 2 tablespoons sugar. Mix until
well combined. Place milk in a large glass measuring cup
and heat in microwave for 1 to 1½ minutes, until heated
throughout, being careful not to boil. Pour 1 cup hot milk
into each mug, stirring constantly until hot cocoa mixture
is completely dissolved. Stir ¼ teaspoon vanilla into each
mug and serve.

WHITE HOT CHOCOLATE
Makes 4 servings

6 (1 oz.) squares white
  chocolate, chopped
¼ tsp. cayenne pepper

½ tsp. cinnamon
1 egg, beaten
3¼ C. milk, divided

In a double boiler over medium heat, melt chopped white chocolate. Heat, stirring frequently, until chocolate is completely melted and smooth. Stir in cayenne pepper and cinnamon. Whisk in beaten egg, mixing until smooth. Gradually add 1 cup milk and continue to heat, whisking constantly, for 2 minutes. Gradually add remaining 2¼ cups milk and stir until heated throughout. Be careful not to simmer or boil milk. Divide hot mixture evenly into four mugs. If desired, garnish with additional cinnamon on top.

CHOCOLATE CARAMEL CAPPUCCINOS

Makes 4 servings

2 C. water
1½ C. milk
¼ C. chocolate syrup

6 T. caramel topping
2 T. instant coffee granules

In a large glass measuring cup or bowl, place water, milk, chocolate syrup, caramel topping and instant coffee granules. Microwave on high for 2 to 3 minutes, stirring after every minute, until thoroughly heated. Remove mixture from microwave and stir well. Pour hot liquid into four coffee mugs.

CHOCOLATE BUZZ
MILKSHAKES

Makes 4 servings

2 C. milk
10 ice cubes
2 oz. brewed espresso
1½ C. chocolate ice cream

4 tsp. instant hot
    chocolate mix
¼ C. chocolate syrup

In a blender, combine milk, ice cubes and espresso. Blend until smooth and add chocolate ice cream, instant hot chocolate mix and chocolate syrup. Blend until fully incorporated. Pour blended milk shakes into 4 glasses.

CHOCOLATE MARTINI
Makes 2 servings

4 oz. dark Crème de Cacao
  or Kahlua
3 oz. vodka
Ice

1 (1 oz.) square semi-sweet
  chocolate, grated
Chocolate syrup, optional

In a cocktail shaker, combine Crème de Cacao and vodka. Add ice and shake vigorously. Strain mixture into two chilled martini glasses. Garnish with grated chocolate. If desired, drizzle a little chocolate syrup over martinis.

COCOA COFFEE KISS

Makes 2 servings

½ oz. Kahlua
½ oz. Irish cream liqueur
6 oz. Crème de Cacao
2 tsp. Grand Marnier
2 C. hot brewed coffee, divided

4 T. whipped topping, divided
2 T. chocolate syrup, divided
2 maraschino cherries, divided

Into a cocktail shaker, pour Kahlua, Irish cream liqueur, Crème de Cacao and Grand Marnier. Shake vigorously and pour evenly into two coffee mugs. Pour 1 cup hot brewed coffee into each mug and mix well. Top each serving with 2 tablespoons whipped topping, 1 tablespoon chocolate syrup and 1 maraschino cherry.

THE CACAO TREE

The cacao tree has the special honor of growing the pods, which hold the beans, which give chocolate its one-of-a-kind flavor. Cacao trees grow melon-like fruits, the pods, which are harvested by hand. Each pod holds 20 to 40 seeds, also known as the cacao beans.

Naturally, cacao trees grow under the shade of the heavy rainforest canopy and require a deep, slightly acidic, moist and well-drained soil. These trees thrive in a consistent climate, with temperatures of 21° to 32° C (70° to 90° F) year round.

Cacao trees are native to northwestern South America, where the largest number of species of the tree are found. However, more than half of the world's supply of commercial cacao comes from the East African countries of Cote D'Ivoire, which exports 41%, and Ghana, which provides 13% of the world's supply.

Indonesia exports 11% of the world's cacao beans. Other cacao exporting countries include Brazil, Cameroon, Ecuador, Madagascar, Nigeria, Sri Lanka, and Venezuela. Cacao is also cultivated for export in Columbia, Congo/

Zaire, Costa Rica, Cuba, Dominican Republic, Fiji, Gabon, Grenada, Haiti, Jamaica, Malaysia, south central Mexico, Panama, Papua New Guinea, Peru, Philippines, Sau Tome, Sierra Leone, Togo, Trinidad and Western Samoa.

PEPPERMINT STEAMER
Makes 1 (8 ounce) serving

2½ to 3 peppermint
patties, unwrapped

1 C. milk, divided
Cocoa powder, optional

Break peppermint patties into pieces. In an 8 ounce mug, place candy pieces and 2 to 3 teaspoons milk. Microwave on high for 30 seconds, remove from microwave and stir. If necessary, return to microwave for heating, 15 seconds at a time, stirring after each heating until candy is melted and mixture is smooth. Slowly stir in remaining milk and return to microwave for 1 additional minute. If desired, garnish with cocoa powder and serve immediately.

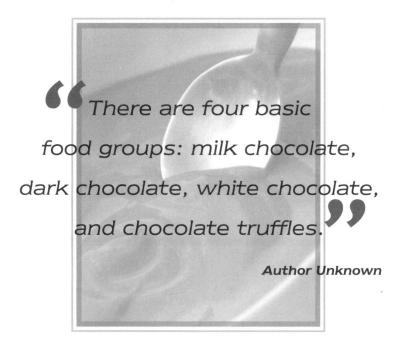

"*There are four basic food groups: milk chocolate, dark chocolate, white chocolate, and chocolate truffles.*"

Author Unknown

CINNAMON MOCHA

Makes 1 serving

1½ to 2 T. chocolate malted
  milk candies
1½ to 2 tsp. instant
  powdered coffee

¾ C. boiling water
1 C. vanilla ice cream
Pinch of cinnamon

In a large coffee mug, combine chocolate malted milk candies and instant powdered coffee. Stir in boiling water, mixing until well blended. Top with vanilla ice cream and stir until well combined. Garnish with a pinch of cinnamon and serve immediately.

RASPBERRY HOT COCOA
Makes 4 cups

2 C. heavy cream
1 C. whole milk
2 T. sugar
⅛ tsp. salt
6 (1 oz.) squares bitter-
  sweet chocolate, chopped

1 T. butter
Whipped cream, optional
Raspberries, optional

In a 1½-quart saucepan over medium heat, combine heavy cream, whole milk, sugar and salt. Bring just to a boil, stirring constantly, and mix in chopped chocolate and butter. Reduce heat to low and continue to heat, stirring frequently, until chocolate is completely melted and mixture is smooth. Ladle hot chocolate into small mugs and, if desired, garnish each serving with whipped topping and raspberries.

CARAMEL-SWIRL COCOA

Makes 6 servings

5 C. water
5 (3 oz.) milk chocolate
  bars, chopped
1¼ C. chilled heavy cream,
  divided

1 T. powdered sugar
3 T. caramel sauce

In a medium saucepan over medium high heat, place water and chopped chocolate. Bring to a simmer, stirring constantly, until chocolate is completely dissolved. Stir in ¼ cup heavy cream. In a medium mixing bowl, beat remaining 1 cup heavy cream at medium high speed until soft peaks form. Drizzle caramel sauce over whipped cream and swirl together lightly to form streaks. Divide hot chocolate liquid evenly into 6 mugs and top each serving with a generous amount of caramel whipped cream.

CHOCOBERRY SPLASH

Makes 1 (12 ounce) serving

¾ C. milk
3 T. frozen sliced
   strawberries, thawed
2 T. chocolate syrup

1 C. plus 2 T. vanilla
   ice cream, divided
1 C. crushed ice
2 T. carbonated water

In a blender, combine milk, thawed strawberries, chocolate syrup and 2 tablespoons vanilla ice cream. Process at medium speed until mixture is smooth. Pour into a tall glass filled with ice. Stir in club soda until well blended. Top mixture with remaining 1 cup ice cream. If desired, garnish with additional sliced strawberries and serve immediately.

CHOCOLATE AND LOVE

Why is it that chocolate and love just seem to go together?

Most likely, you have either received or given chocolate to someone you love. More than half of all gifts given on Valentine's Day contain chocolate. It is interesting, then, that chocolate has never been proven to be an aphrodisiac, but has filled that role for many.

The association may have generated from that feeling of well-being that many people experience when eating chocolate (which is explained further on page 34). It could also be because chocolate is often considered a treat, something that people enjoy and cherish. These feelings have proven aphrodisiac effects.

Most likely, the connection between love and chocolate is culturally inherited. If the association is made early in life it will continue to be made, and be passed along to future generations.

Another belief on the connection between chocolate and love, is revealed in the pod of the cacao tree. When cut crosswise, it resembles a heart.

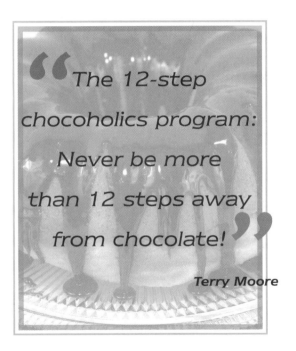

The 12-step chocoholics program: Never be more than 12 steps away from chocolate!

Terry Moore

MEXICAN SPICE HOT CHOCOLATE

Makes 3 to 4 servings

3 (1 oz.) squares bitter-sweet chocolate, chopped
3 C. milk
2 T. sugar

Pinch of salt
Miniature marshmallows, optional
Cinnamon sticks, optional

In a medium saucepan over medium low heat, combine the chopped chocolate, milk, sugar and salt. Heat, stirring frequently, until chocolate is completely melted and milk is very hot, about 10 minutes. Be careful not to boil. Remove from the heat and, using a wire whisk, beat milk mixture until frothy. Divide hot chocolate evenly into mugs. If desired, top each serving with a few marshmallows and serve with cinnamon sticks as garnish.

FROZEN COCOA
Makes 6 servings

½ C. cocoa powder   2¾ C. low-fat 1% milk
¾ C. sugar

In a small saucepan over low heat, combine cocoa powder and sugar. Stir in just enough milk to form a smooth paste. Once texture is achieved, stir in all but 2 tablespoons of the remaining milk. Continue to heat, stirring frequently, until mixture is warm and sugar is completely dissolved. Transfer mixture to a shallow container or pour into ice cube trays. Cover and place in freezer for 6 hours or overnight. Mixture can be frozen up to 2 weeks. To serve, break into chunks using a fork or knife. Transfer frozen mixture to a blender or food processor. Add remaining 2 tablespoons milk and process on high until mixture is smooth but thick and lighter in color. Transfer mixture to serving glasses, frosted goblets or bowls and serve immediately.

ICY CARAMEL PARFAITS

Makes 8 servings

½ C. whole milk
1½ C. heavy cream, divided
3 T. water
¾ C. sugar, divided
8 large egg yolks

7 (1 oz.) squares
    bittersweet chocolate,
    melted and cooled
½ tsp. vanilla

In a small heavy saucepan over medium heat, bring milk and ½ cup heavy cream just to a boil, stirring constantly. Remove from heat, cover and keep warm. In a separate small heavy saucepan, bring water and ½ cup sugar to a boil, stirring until sugar is completely dissolved. Bring mixture to a boil. Gently swirl pan over heat until mixture is a deep golden caramel, but do not stir. Remove from heat and carefully add warm cream mixture. The mixture should steam vigorously and the caramel will harden. Reduce heat to low and continue to heat, whisking occasionally, until caramel is dissolved. In a metal bowl, whisk together egg yolks, remaining ¼ cup sugar and salt. Slowly add hot caramel mixture and whisk well. Transfer mixture to a saucepan and place over low heat, stirring frequently, until thickened and mixture reaches 170° on a candy thermometer. Be careful not to let mixture boil. Pour custard through a fine-hole sieve into a mixing bowl. Beat at high speed for about 10 minutes. Add melted chocolate and vanilla. Beat remaining 1 cup heavy cream at high speed until stiff peaks form. Whisk ¼ of the whipped cream into the chocolate mixture. Gently fold in remaining whipped cream. Mix thoroughly and divide mixture evenly into 8 paper cupcake liners, smoothing the tops. Cover each cup with aluminum foil and place in freezer for at least 12 hours. To serve, carefully tear off each paper cup and invert parfaits onto serving plates.

" I have this theory that chocolate slows down the aging process.... It may not be true, but do I dare take the chance? "

Author Unknown

CHOCOLATE CHIP COFFEE CAKE

Makes 12 servings

2 large egg whites

$^1/_3$ C. brown sugar

1 tsp. salt, divided

1½ C. coarsely chopped walnuts

1¼ C. miniature chocolate chips, divided

2 C. cake flour

¼ tsp. baking powder

¼ tsp. baking soda

1 C. plus 2 T. sugar

½ C. butter, softened

3 whole eggs

¾ C. plus 2 T. sour cream, divided

¾ C. powdered sugar

Preheat oven to 350°. Thoroughly grease and flour a 10″ tube pan and coat with non-stick cooking spray. In a medium bowl, combine egg whites, brown sugar and ½ teaspoon salt. Mix well and stir in chopped walnuts and ¼ cup chocolate chips. In a separate bowl, combine cake flour, remaining ½ teaspoon salt, baking powder and baking soda. In a large mixing bowl, beat together sugar and butter at medium high speed until well blended. Beat in whole eggs, one at a time. Alternating, slowly fold in flour mixture and ¾ cup sour cream, mixing well after each addition. Stir in remaining 1 cup chocolate chips. Mix until well combined and transfer mixture to prepared pan. Sprinkle walnut and chocolate chip mixture evenly over batter. Bake cake in oven for about 1 hour, or until a toothpick inserted in center of cake comes out clean. Remove cake from oven and let cool on wire racks for about 10 minutes. Meanwhile, in a small bowl, combine remaining 2 tablespoons sour cream and powdered sugar. Turn cake out onto rack and drizzle powdered sugar mixture over cake.

"Strength is the capacity
to break a chocolate
bar into four pieces with
your bare hands – and then
eat just one of the pieces."

Judith Viorst

PUPS BEWARE

You may have heard that it is not a good idea to feed chocolate to animals. Not only is it a bad idea, but it may be fatal. A chemical, theobromine, present in chocolate has been found to poison dogs, even in small amounts. Though cats are not as susceptible to the chemical, it is always best to keep chocolate away from all pets.

In most cases, it would take 100 to 150 milligrams of theobromide per kilogram of body weight to cause a toxic reaction in a dog. Other variables, such as individual sensitivity, animal size and chocolate concentration must also be considered.

On average, milk chocolate contains 44 milligrams of theobromine per ounce, while semi-sweet chocolate contains 150 milligrams per ounce and baker's unsweetened chocolate contains 390 milligrams per ounce.

COCOA SPICE SEASONING RUB

Makes about 1²/₃ cups

8 T. paprika
½ tsp. cayenne pepper
5 T. pepper
6 T. onion powder
3 T. salt

2½ T. dried oregano
2½ T. dried thyme
3 T. toffee bits, crushed
3 T. cocoa powder

In a medium bowl, combine paprika, cayenne pepper, pepper, onion powder, salt, oregano, thyme, crushed toffee bits and powder. Mix until well combined and transfer to an airtight container. Store in a cool, dry place for up to 6 weeks. Use mixture as a seasoning or rub for poultry, pork, beef, seafood, salad, soups or vegetables, or use in recipes on pages 31 and 60.

CARRIBBEAN CHUTNEY

Makes about 3 cups

1 firm mango
1 firm fresh peach
1 T. butter
1 T. olive oil
½ C. pineapple, diced
½ C. caramelized red onions

⅛ tsp. curry powder
⅛ tsp. ground ginger
¼ tsp. Cocoa Spice
  Seasoning Rub
  (recipe on page 30)
¼ C. chocolate chips

Peel, halve and seed the mango and peach. Cut mango and peach flesh into ½″ cubes and set aside. In a medium saucepan over medium heat, combine butter and olive oil. Heat, stirring occasionally, until butter is melted. Add mango, peach and pineapple pieces and sauté until tender but firm. Stir in caramelized onions. Add curry powder, ground ginger and prepared Cocoa Spice Seasoning Rub. Stir gently and transfer mixture to a serving bowl. Let cool completely before stirring in chocolate chips. Mix until evenly blended, cover and store in refrigerator until ready to serve.

DOUBLE CHOCOLATE PUDDING
Makes 4 cups

¼ C. cornstarch
6 T. sugar
3 T. cocoa powder
¼ tsp. cinnamon, optional
1 T. espresso powder, optional
Pinch of salt
Pinch of cayenne pepper,
  optional

1¼ C. heavy cream
1¼ C. milk
7 (1 oz.) squares
  bittersweet chocolate,
  finely chopped
1½ T. butter, cut into pieces

In a medium saucepan, combine cornstarch, sugar, cocoa powder, cinnamon, espresso powder, salt and cayenne pepper. Heat, stirring occasionally with a wire whisk. In a measuring cup, mix together heavy cream and milk. Mix 1 cup cream mixture into dry ingredients in saucepan, stirring until cornstarch is completely dissolved. Mix in remaining cream mixture and increase heat to medium high. Continue to heat, stirring constantly, until mixture begins to boil and thicken, about 5 minutes. Stir in finely chopped chocolate and heat for 1 additional minute, whisking continuously. Remove saucepan from heat and stir in butter pieces, mixing until butter is completely melted. Transfer mixture to a bowl and cover with plastic wrap, letting plastic rest directly on pudding mixture to prevent a skin from forming on the surface. Let pudding stand for about 45 minutes, until temperature is lukewarm. Transfer pudding to serving bowls or goblets and serve immediately. If chilled pudding is desired, cover pudding bowls with plastic wrap, with plastic resting on surface of the pudding, and place in refrigerator for up to 24 hours.

"Chocolate doesn't make the world go around ... but it certainly makes the ride worthwhile!"

Author Unknown

THE FEEL GOOD EFFECT

Despite its taste-bud-delighting flavor, many people report that their enjoyment in eating chocolate rests in the "good feeling" they experience after indulging in the treat. Scientists have found that chocolate contains more than 300 known chemicals. Unfortunately, they can only speculate which chemicals or chemical compounds explain this pleasurable side effect of consuming chocolate.

While caffeine is the most well known chemical found in chocolate, it is only present in small quantities. A weak stimulant, theobromine, is also found within the chemical make-up of chocolate. The combination of these two chemicals could provide the "pick up" chocolate consumers experience.

Another chemical found in chocolate, phenylethylamine, is related to amphetamines, which are strong stimulants. These stimulates have been known to increase the activity of neurotransmitters in the part of the brain that controls the ability to pay attention and stay alert.

Perhaps the most controversial theory as to why chocolate makes people feel good surrounds the findings of researches at the Neurosciences Institute in San Diego. The scientists believe that chocolate contains pharmacologically active substances that have the same effect on the brain as marijuana, which may help explain the sometimes seemingly drug-induced psychoses associated with chocolate cravings.

> "*Researchers have discovered that chocolate produces some of the same reactions in the brain as marijuana. The researchers also discovered other similarities between the two, but can't remember what they are.*"

Matt Lauer on NBC's "The Today Show"

BLISSFUL WALDORF SALAD

Makes 6 to 8 servings

¼ C. mayonnaise
1 T. sugar
2 T. raisins
1 tsp. finely grated
  orange peel
2 C. Red Delicious
  apples, chopped

½ C. mandarin orange
  segments
½ C. finely chopped celery
½ C. chopped walnuts
½ C. miniature
  chocolate chips
Salad greens

In a medium bowl, combine mayonnaise, sugar, raisins and grated orange peel. Fold in chopped apples, mandarin orange segments, finely chopped celery, chopped walnuts and miniature chocolate chips. Mix until well blended and drizzle over salad greens. Toss until dressing is evenly incorporated. Store leftovers in an airtight container in refrigerator.

CARAMELIZED MACADAMIA NUTS

Makes 10 to 12 servings

1 C. sugar
2 C. whole macadamia nuts

1 lb. bittersweet chocolate, chopped
½ C. powdered sugar

In a saucepan over high heat, combine sugar and macadamia nuts. Heat, stirring constantly with a wooden spoon, until the sugar melts and the nuts become white and coated, about 12 minutes. Transfer nuts to a parchment-lined baking sheet and set aside to cool slightly. Once nuts are cool enough to handle, separate any clusters and let nuts cool completely. In a double boiler over boiling water, melt chopped chocolate. Place nuts in melted chocolate and stir until nuts are completely coated. Place chocolate-covered nuts on parchment-lined baking sheets to cool. Place baking sheets in refrigerator until chocolate has hardened. If any melted chocolate remains, coat nuts again in chocolate, place on baking sheets and cool in refrigerator. Using a sifter, sift powdered sugar over chocolate covered nuts. Roll nuts lightly to coat with powdered sugar and store in an airtight container.

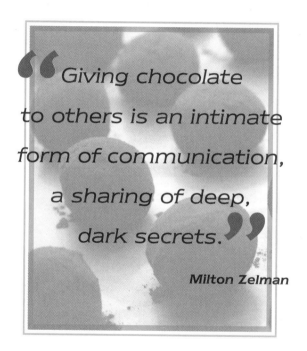

Giving chocolate to others is an intimate form of communication, a sharing of deep, dark secrets.

Milton Zelman

MOCHA BBQ SAUCE

Makes about 3 cups

1 C. strong brewed coffee
1 C. Worcestershire sauce
1 C. ketchup
½ C. white vinegar
¼ C. brown sugar
3 T. chili powder

2 C. chopped Vidalia onions
6 cloves garlic, crushed
2 tsp. salt
6 T. dark syrup
3 T. cocoa powder

In a large saucepan over medium heat, combine strong brewed coffee, Worcestershire sauce, ketchup, vinegar, brown sugar, chili powder and chopped Vidalia onions. Stir in crushed garlic, salt, dark syrup and cocoa powder. Mix thoroughly until well combined. Heat, stirring occasionally, until mixture begins to simmer. Let simmer for 20 to 25 minutes, being careful not to boil. Remove sauce from heat and let cool. Serve with beef, chicken or pork or use in recipes calling for BBQ sauce. Store sauce in an airtight container in refrigerator for up to 3 weeks.

ALMOND CHOCOLATE SQUARES

Makes 4 squares

2 T. almond butter
2 slices white bread
½ banana, sliced

1 T. chocolate hazelnut
spread

Spread an even amount of almond butter over one side of one bread slice. Arrange sliced bananas over almond butter. Spread chocolate hazelnut spread over one side of remaining bread slice. Place slice over bananas, spread side down, forming a sandwich. Cut sandwich into 4 squares and serve.

PEANUT BUTTER CHOCOLATE BANANA YOGURT

Makes 5 servings

¼ C. peanut butter
2 (1 oz.) squares
   semi-sweet chocolate
1 medium banana, mashed

12 oz. evaporated milk
½ C. sugar
½ tsp. vanilla
1 C. low-fat vanilla yogurt

In a double boiler over boiling water, place chocolate squares. Heat, stirring occasionally, until chocolate is completely melted. In a medium bowl, combine melted chocolate, peanut butter and mashed banana. Stir in evaporated milk, sugar and vanilla. Fold in yogurt. Transfer mixture to an electric ice cream maker and follow manufacturer's directions to make frozen yogurt.

This recipe requires an electric ice cream maker.

"There's nothing better than a good friend, except a good friend with chocolate."

Linda Grayson

THE RULES OF CHOCOLATE

- If you have melted chocolate all over your hands, you're eating it too slowly. Eat your chocolate faster.

- Raisins, cherries, orange slices and strawberries covered in chocolate still count as fruit. Eat as many as you want.

- If you need to get two pounds of chocolate home from the store in a hot car, the only solution is to eat it all in the parking lot.

- To achieve a balanced diet, eat equal amounts of dark and white chocolate.

- Place "eat chocolate" at the top of your list of things to do today. That way, at least you will get one thing done.

BLUEBERRY WHITE CHIP MUFFINS

Makes 1½ dozen

2¼ C. flour, divided
½ C. plus ⅓ C. sugar, divided
¼ C. brown sugar
2½ tsp. baking powder
½ tsp. salt
¼ C. plus 3 T. butter or margarine, divided

¾ C. milk
1 large egg, lightly beaten
½ tsp. grated lemon peel
1 (12 oz.) pkg. white chocolate chips, divided
1½ C. fresh or frozen blueberries
¼ tsp. cinnamon

Preheat oven to 375°. Line 18 muffin cups with paper liners. In a large bowl, combine 2 cups flour, ½ cup sugar, brown sugar, baking powder and salt. Mix until well combined. In a microwave-safe dish, place ¼ cup butter. Heat butter in microwave until melted. Add milk, beaten egg, melted butter and lemon peel to flour mixture. Fold 1½ cups white chocolate chips and blueberries into batter. Mix gently and spoon mixture evenly into prepared muffin cups, filling each cup ¾ full of batter. To prepare streusel topping, in a small bowl, combine remaining $\frac{1}{3}$ cup sugar, remaining ¼ cup flour and cinnamon. Using a pastry blender, cut butter into cinnamon mixture until coarse crumbs form. Sprinkle mixture over batter in muffin cups. Bake in oven for 22 to 25 minutes, or until a toothpick inserted in center of muffins comes out clean. Remove muffin pans from oven and set on wire racks. Let muffins cool in pans for about 5 minutes. Meanwhile, place remaining white chocolate chips in a small, heavy-duty ziplock bag. Close bag and place in microwave for about 30 seconds. Remove bag from microwave and knead by hand until white chocolate is melted and smooth. Cut a small corner off of the bag and pipe melted chocolate over muffins. Serve warm.

BREAD MACHINE
BROWNIE BREAD

Makes 1 (1 pound) loaf

½ C. cocoa powder
½ C. boiling water
2½ tsp. active dry yeast
⅔ C. plus 2 tsp. sugar, divided
½ C. warm water

3 C. bread flour
⅔ C. sugar
1 tsp. salt
2 T. vegetable oil
1 egg
1 egg yolk

In a small bowl, combine cocoa powder and boiling water, mixing until cocoa powder is completely dissolved. In a separate bowl, dissolve yeast and 2 teaspoons sugar in warm water. Set mixture aside until creamy, about 10 minutes. Place cocoa mixture, yeast mixture, bread flour, remaining ⅔ cup sugar, salt, vegetable oil, egg and egg yolk in bread machine pan. Select the Basic bread cycle and press Start.

CHOCOLATE CINNAMON ROLLS

Makes 1 dozen rolls

2 (1 lb.) loaves frozen white
   yeast bread dough
¼ C. sugar
1 T. cinnamon
1 (12 oz.) pkg. chocolate
   chips

1 C. chopped nuts
1 C. powdered sugar, sifted
4 tsp. milk

Preheat oven to 350°. Grease two 9″ round baking pans. On a floured flat surface, roll one dough loaf into a 10 x 16″ rectangle. In a bowl, combine sugar and cinnamon. Sprinkle mixture over dough to within ½″ of the edge. Sprinkle 1 cup chocolate chips and ½ cup nuts over dough. Roll dough into a log, starting from the short end. Pinch the ends to seal the dough. Cut log into 6 slices and place rounds, cut side up, in one of the prepared baking pans. Repeat with remaining bread loaf, sugar mixture, chocolate chips and nuts. Place rounds in remaining baking pan. Cover pans with towels and place in a warm place to rise, until dough almost fills the pans. Bake for 25 to 30 minutes, or until golden brown. Let rolls cool slightly. To prepare glaze, combine sifted sugar and milk. Mix well and drizzle over warm rolls.

WACKY WAFFLES

Makes 4 servings

1¼ C. Bisquick baking mix
¼ C. cocoa powder
½ C. sugar
1 C. buttermilk
1 large egg

1 T. vegetable oil
½ C. chocolate M&M's
   baking bits
Powdered sugar and
   maple syrup

Preheat waffle iron. In large bowl, combine baking mix, cocoa powder, sugar, buttermilk, egg and vegetable oil. Stir until well combined. Spoon about ½ cup of the batter mixture onto hot waffle iron. Sprinkle about 2 tablespoons M&M's baking bits over batter in waffle iron and close the lid. Bake waffle for about 1 to 2 minutes, or until the steaming stops. Place waffle on serving plate and sprinkle with powdered sugar. Serve immediately with maple syrup and additional M&M's baking bits. Repeat with remaining batter.

CREAM SCONES
Makes 8 to 12 scones

2 C. flour
¼ C. plus 1 T. sugar, divided
2½ tsp. baking powder
½ tsp. salt

3 (1 oz.) squares bitter-
sweet or semi-sweet
chocolate, chopped
1½ C. heavy cream, divided

Preheat oven to 425°. In a large bowl, combine flour, ¼ cup sugar, baking powder and salt. Mix until well combined and fold in chopped chocolate. Stir lightly, forming a well in center of dry mixture. Pour 1¼ cups heavy cream into well. Mix well, scraping sides of bowl. Continue to fold batter until smooth. Turn out dough onto a lightly floured flat surface. Pat dough into an 8″ round, about ¾″ thick. Cut round into 8 to 12 wedges. Place wedges 1″ apart on a parchment-lined baking sheet. Brush remaining ¼ cup heavy cream over tops of scones and sprinkle with remaining 1 tablespoon sugar. Bake until tops are golden brown, about 12 to 15 minutes. Remove from oven and let cool on a rack. Serve warm or at room temperature.

" *All of the evil that people have thrust upon chocolate is really more deserved by milk chocolate, which is essentially contaminated. The closer you get to a pure chocolate liquor, the purer it is, the more satisfying it is, the safer it is, and the healthier it is.* "

Arnold Ismach

TYPES OF CHOCOLATE

Unsweetened Chocolate: chocolate liquor that has been solidified into blocks used for baking.

Semi-sweet or Bittersweet Chocolate: a dark chocolate containing a minimum of 35% chocolate liquor. This type of chocolate may also contain cocoa butter, vanilla and sugar.

Sweet or Dark Chocolate: chocolate that has a minimum of 15% chocolate liquor. The amount of sweeteners and cocoa butter added vary depending on the manufacturer.

Milk Chocolate: chocolate containing milk solids and at least 10% chocolate liquor.

White Chocolate: despite popular belief, this is not technically a chocolate, as it contains no chocolate liquor. It is made up of mostly cocoa butter, milk solids, sweetener and flavorings.

STUFFED CINNAMON FRENCH TOAST

Makes 6 servings

1 loaf day-old French bread
1 C. milk chocolate chips
5 eggs, beaten
1¼ C. milk

¼ tsp. cinnamon
¼ tsp. vanilla
Maple syrup or whipped
  topping, optional

Coat a 9 x 13″ baking dish with non-stick cooking spray. Cut French bread into six ½″ thick slices. Cut 2″ long slits into one side of each bread slice, cutting ¾ of the way through bread to create a pocket. Spoon 2 tablespoons chocolate chips into pocket of each bread slice, pressing to enclose chocolate. Place filled slices in prepared baking pan. Whisk together beaten eggs, milk, cinnamon and vanilla. Mix well and pour mixture over bread slices in baking dish. Cover dish and place in refrigerator for 2 hours or overnight. Preheat oven to 400°. Bake, uncovered, for 20 to 25 minutes, or until French toast is golden brown. If desired, serve with maple syrup or whipped topping.

PUMPKIN CHOCOLATE CHIP BREAD
Makes 3 loaves

3 C. sugar
1 (15 oz.) can
  pumpkin puree
1 C. vegetable oil
²/₃ C. water
4 eggs
3½ C. flour
1 T. cinnamon

1 T. nutmeg
2 tsp. baking soda
1½ tsp. salt
1 C. miniature chocolate
  chips
½ C. chopped walnuts,
  optional

Preheat oven to 350°. Thoroughly grease and flour three
5 x 9″ loaf pans. In a large bowl, combine sugar, pumpkin
puree, vegetable oil, water and eggs. Beat at medium high
speed until smooth. Stir in flour, cinnamon, nutmeg, baking
soda and salt. Mix well and gently fold in chocolate chips
and walnuts. Divide mixture into prepared pans. Bake in
oven for 1 hour, or until a toothpick inserted in center of
loaves comes out clean. Let loaves cool in baking pans
before turning out onto wire racks.

"*It's not that chocolates are a substitute for love. Love is a substitute for chocolate. Chocolate is, let's face it, far more reliable than a man.*"

Miranda Ingram

COCOA ROUND BREAD
Makes 2 loaves

1 T. sunflower seed oil	6 C. bread flour
2 tsp. salt	4½ T. sugar
1¾ C. warm water	¾ C. cocoa powder
(at least 110°)	
1 (¼ oz.) pkg. instant yeast	

Preheat oven to 425°. In a large bowl, combine sunflower seed oil, salt, warm water, instant yeast, bread flour, sugar and cocoa powder. Mix well, using a wooden spoon, until a soft dough forms. Turn out dough onto a flat floured surface. Knead dough for 5 minutes, until dough is smooth and elastic. Divide dough into two equal parts and roll each half into a ball. Place each ball on a greased baking sheet. Using a sharp knife, cut a criss-cross pattern in the top of each ball and cover with a kitchen towel. Let dough rise until doubled in size. Bake loaves for 35 minutes. Remove from oven and let cool slightly before removing from baking sheets to wire racks.

CHOCOLATE SURPRISE MUFFINS

Makes 1 dozen muffins

2 C. flour
¾ C. sugar
¼ C. cocoa powder
3 tsp. baking powder
½ tsp. salt
½ tsp. cinnamon
1 egg

1 C. milk
⅓ C. vegetable oil
¼ C. instant powdered milk
2 T. hot water
1 tsp. butter, softened
¼ tsp. almond extract
1 C. shredded coconut

Preheat oven to 400°. Lightly grease 12 muffin cups. In a large bowl, combine flour, sugar, cocoa powder, baking powder, salt and cinnamon. In a small bowl, lightly beat egg, using a wire whisk, and stir in milk and vegetable oil. Make a well in the center of the flour mixture and add egg mixture, stirring until batter is moistened. Pour batter into prepared muffin cups. In a small bowl, combine powdered milk and hot water, stirring until well blended. Mix in butter, almond extract and coconut. Form mixture into 12 balls. Push 1 ball lightly into the batter in each muffin cup. Bake for 20 to 25 minutes.

"Chemically speaking, chocolate really is the world's perfect food."

Michael Levine

CHOCOLATE MAYAN CHICKEN
Makes 4 servings

1 (14 oz.) can sweetened condensed milk

3 T. chicken bouillon granules, divided

4 bone-in chicken breast halves

6 T. vegetable oil, divided

½ C. diced onions

½ C. diced carrots

¼ C. diced celery

2 red chili peppers, halved and seeded

2 large cloves garlic, peeled and minced

1 shallot, peeled and minced

1 sprig fresh rosemary

2 sprigs fresh thyme

2 bay leaves

5 juniper berries, crushed

10 whole peppercorns

3 whole cloves

1 cinnamon stick

2¼ C. dry red wine, divided

1 C. chicken broth

2 (1 oz.) squares semi-sweet chocolate, grated

Preheat oven to 425°. In a large bowl, combine sweetened condensed milk and 2 tablespoons chicken bouillon granules. Place chicken breasts in same bowl and turn until all sides of chicken breasts are coated with bouillon mixture. Cover bowl with plastic wrap and place in refrigerator for 5 hours or overnight. On the stovetop, place a roasting pan over medium high heat and add 4 tablespoons vegetable oil. Add diced onions, diced carrots, diced celery, chili pepper halves, minced garlic and minced shallot to roasting pan. Add sprig of rosemary, sprigs of thyme, bay leaves, crushed juniper berries, whole peppercorns, whole cloves and cinnamon stick to ingredients in roasting pan. Heat, turning occasionally, until vegetables are evenly browned. Stir in 1 cup red wine. Cover roasting pan and place in preheated oven for 25 minutes. Gradually mix in remaining red wine during this time. Stir in chicken broth and continue to heat in oven for 1 hour. Carefully remove roasting pan from oven and pour mixture through a metal sieve into a medium saucepan, removing any solids. Heat liquid mixture over medium low heat until liquid has reduced to a sauce. Stir in grated chocolate, mixing until chocolate is completely melted and smooth. In a large skillet over medium high heat, place remaining 2 tablespoons vegetable oil. Remove chicken breast from refrigerator and season with remaining 1 tablespoon chicken bouillon granules, covering all sides generously. Cook chicken breasts in skillet, turning once, to brown on both sides. Once chicken breasts are cooked throughout, remove chicken breasts to serving platter and pour hot sauce over chicken and serve immediately.

COCOA SPICED SALMON FILET

1 firm mango
1 firm peach
1 T. butter
1 T. olive oil
½ C. diced pineapple
½ C. red onion, caramelized
⅛ tsp. curry powder

⅛ tsp. ground ginger
¼ tsp. Cocoa Spice
   Seasoning Rub
   (recipe on page 30)
¼ C. chocolate chips
2 large salmon filets

Preheat oven to 400°. Peel, halve and seed the mango and peach. Cut mango and peach flesh into ½″ cubes and set aside. In a large saucepan over medium heat, place butter and olive oil. Heat, stirring occasionally, until butter is melted. Add cubed mango, cubed peach and diced pineapple. Sauté fruits until tender and stir in caramelized onion. Mix in curry powder, ground ginger and Cocoa Spice Seasoning Rub. Stir lightly and transfer mixture to a medium bowl. Let mixture cool completely and stir in miniature chocolate chips, mixing until blended. Cover and place in refrigerator until ready to serve. Coat two baking sheets with non-stick cooking spray and place 1 salmon filet, skin-side-down, on each baking sheet. Lightly coat each salmon filet with cooking spray. Sprinkle an additional 1 teaspoon Cocoa Spice Seasoning Rub over each filet. Bake in oven for about 20 to 30 minutes, or until salmon flakes easily with a fork. Remove from oven and place salmon filets on serving platter. Spoon pineapple mixture over filets and serve immediately.

Life is like a box of chocolates

– you never know

what you're going to get.

Forrest Gump

PULLED BEEF & PORK
Makes 16 to 20 servings

2 (2 lb.) boneless beef
chuck roasts

8 country-style pork ribs

8 T. vegetable oil, divided

Salt and pepper to taste

2 T. plus 4 tsp. ground
cumin, divided

1 C. mild chili powder

4 tsp. dried oregano

4 large onions, diced

2 (28 oz.) cans crushed
tomatoes

1 (16 oz.) can crushed
tomatoes

12 cloves garlic, minced

2 (1 oz.) squares bitter-
sweet chocolate,
coarsely chopped

4 (15½ oz.) cans pinto
or kidney beans, rinsed,
optional

Preheat oven to 450°. Using paper towels, thoroughly pat dry
beef chuck roasts and pork ribs. Place a large, heavy roasting
pan over medium heat, covering two burners on stovetop. In a
medium bowl, place 2 tablespoons vegetable oil. Place half of
the meat in bowl and turn to coat. Sprinkle salt, pepper and 1
tablespoon ground cumin over meat. Place meat in roasting pan
and increase to medium high heat. Cook, turning once or twice,
until browned on all sides. Transfer cooked meat to a large soup
pot. Repeat with remaining meat by coating first in oil, sprin-

kling with salt, pepper and 1 tablespoon ground cumin and then browning in roasting pan. Transfer remaining browned meat to soup pot and set roasting pan aside. Add 2½ cups water to the soup pot and cover with aluminum foil, pressing down so foil touches the browned meat. Seal aluminum foil tightly around the top of the soup pot and place lid on pot. Place soup pot over medium high heat and cook until you can hear juices bubbling in the pan. Place filled pot in preheated oven. Cook for 90 minutes, without opening oven door. Carefully remove soup pot from oven and let cool. The meat should be very tender. Return cooked meat to roasting pan and, using two forks, shred pork and beef into smaller pieces, discarding the pork bones. Pour meat juices from soup pot and roasting pan into a large measuring cup. Add enough water to equal 12 cups. Meanwhile, in a medium skillet over low heat, combine chili powder, dried oregano and remaining 4 teaspoons ground cumin, stirring constantly, until spices are fragrant and darker in color; being careful not to burn. Place roasting pan over medium heat, covering two burners on stovetop and add remaining 4 tablespoons vegetable oil. Stir in diced onions and sauté until softened, about 7 to 8 minutes. Add heated spices, crushed tomatoes, shredded meat and juices. Let mixture simmer, stirring occasionally, for 1 to 1½ hours. Mix in minced garlic, grated chocolate and, if desired, rinsed beans. Let simmer for an additional 5 minutes. Serve shredded meat as is or over hamburger buns.

SPICED CHICKEN WITH SALSA MOLE

Makes 4 servings

2 T. ground coffee beans
2 T. cocoa powder
1 T. salt
1 tsp. chili powder
1 T. brown sugar
1 T. vegetable oil
4 boneless, skinless
  chicken breasts
Cilantro sprigs, optional

1 C. chopped fresh tomatoes
1 avocado, peeled
  and diced
1 green onion, minced
1 clove garlic, minced
1 T. fresh chopped cilantro
¼ C. miniature
  chocolate chips
1 tsp. lime juice

Preheat oven to 425°. Thoroughly grease a baking sheet
and set aside. In a medium bowl, combine coffee beans,
cocoa powder, salt, chili powder and brown sugar. Coat
chicken breasts on all sides with vegetable oil. Place
chicken breasts in bowl and turn until coated in cocoa
mixture. Place coated chicken pieces on prepared baking
sheet. Bake in oven for 20 to 25 minutes, or until juices from

chicken are clear. Meanwhile, in a medium bowl, combine chopped tomatoes, diced avocado, minced green onion, minced garlic, chopped cilantro, miniature chocolate chips and lime juice. To serve, place cooked chicken breasts and salsa mixture on a large platter. If desired, garnish with fresh cilantro sprigs.

"Caramels are only a fad.

Chocolate is a permanent thing."

Milton Snavely Hershey

A FAMOUS AMERICAN CHOCOLATIER

For years, everyone knew that the delicious chocolates of Switzerland, Belgium, France, Germany and Denmark pretty much cornered the market on this famous treat. Then in the late 19th century, an inspired entrepreneur helped the U.S. mark its own name on the world of chocolate.

Milton S. Hershey began his chocolate legacy with a four-year apprenticeship to a candy maker in Lancaster, Pennsylvania. At 19 years of age, Hershey set out to start his own candy business in Philadelphia, but, after six years of hard work, he failed. Hershey turned his attention to caramels and, after another apprenticeship and another failed business, he finally found success with his Lancaster Caramel Company. Before long, Hershey employed 1400 people and was shipping his caramels all over the U.S. and Europe.

It wasn't until 1893, at the age of 36, that Hershey began his fascination with chocolate. At the World's Columbian Exposition in Chicago, Hershey purchased some German machinery and used it to produce a chocolate coating for his caramels at the Lancaster factory. Aware of the growing demand for chocolate, he started the Hershey Chocolate Company. He then spent years perfecting a recipe for milk chocolate, which, up to then, had been a closely guarded secret of the Swiss. Once the formula was ready, Hershey began mass producing and distributing his milk chocolate candy. The world-famous Hershey bar was born.

In 1900, Hershey sold his caramel company and, three years later, moved his growing chocolate company to a spot close to his birthplace in Derry Township. Hershey always believed that people who were treated fairly and who lived in a comfortable, pleasant environment would be better workers. He then set upon building an infrastructure to take care of his employees. Soon, his plans for building housing, churches, parks, recreational facilities and lots of schools were underway. Hershey later saw to it that a community building, department store, convention hall, amusement park, swimming pool and more schools were added to the growing town, appropriately named Hershey, Pennsylvania.

CHICKEN ENCHILADAS IN CHOCOLATE SAUCE

Makes 6 to 8 servings

5 T. vegetable oil, divided

3 cloves garlic, minced, divided

1 tsp. onion, minced

½ tsp. dried oregano

1 T. plus 2½ tsp. chili powder, divided

½ tsp. dried basil

½ tsp. pepper, divided

1¼ tsp. salt, divided

¼ tsp. ground cumin

1 tsp. dried parsley flakes

¼ C. salsa

¾ C. tomato sauce

½ C. chocolate chips

1 1/2 C. water

2 lbs. skinless boneless chicken breasts, cut into strips

1 medium yellow onion, diced

2 T. chopped garlic

1 T. brown sugar

¼ C. fresh chopped cilantro

½ C. chicken broth

5 C. shredded Cheddar cheese, divided

20 corn tortillas

Preheat oven to 375°. Lightly grease two 9 x 13″ baking dishes and set aside. To prepare Chocolate Sauce, in a large saucepan over medium heat, place 1 tablespoon vegetable oil.

Stir in two cloves minced garlic and sauté for 1 to 2 minutes. Mix in minced onion, oregano, 2½ teaspoons chili powder, basil, ½ teaspoon pepper, ¼ teaspoon salt, cumin, dried parsley flakes, salsa, tomato sauce, chocolate chips and water. Bring mixture to a boil, stirring lightly. Reduce heat to low at let simmer for about 15 to 20 minutes. In the meantime, prepare enchiladas. In a large heavy skillet over medium high heat, place remaining 4 tablespoons vegetable oil. Add chicken pieces, diced yellow onion, remaining 1 clove chopped garlic, remaining 1 teaspoon salt and remaining ½ teaspoon pepper. Heat, stirring occasionally, until chicken is browned and onion is softened. Mix in remaining 1 tablespoon chili powder, brown sugar and fresh chopped cilantro. Mix in chicken broth and deglaze pan. Remove from heat and let cool. Remove chicken from skillet and shred meat by pulling apart into small strips and return to skillet. Stir 3 cups shredded Cheddar cheese into skillet. Wrap corn tortillas in damp cloth and microwave on high for 10 to 20 seconds, or until softened. Spoon ⅓ cup chicken mixture into center of each tortilla and roll tightly. Place rolled enchiladas, seam side down, into prepared baking dishes. Pour Chocolate Sauce over rolled enchiladas and sprinkle remaining 2 cups shredded cheese over top. Cover and bake in oven for 20 minutes.

STEAK FILET WITH CHOCOLATE SAUCE

Makes 6 servings

3 C. shaved dark chocolate
4 C. water
2 T. whole grain mustard
1 T. sugar
2 T. vegetable oil

4 lbs. boneless top round steaks
Sour cream, optional
Fresh chopped chives, optional

In a medium saucepan over medium heat, combine shaved dark chocolate, water, whole grain mustard and sugar. Heat, stirring constantly, until mixture is smooth. To prepare steaks, in a large skillet over medium high heat, place vegetable oil. Fry steak in hot oil, turning until browned on both sides and cooked to desired doneness. Remove cooked steaks to serving platter and repeat with remaining steaks, adding more oil as needed. Pour melted chocolate sauce over steaks and serve. If desired, garnish serve with dollops of sour cream and fresh chopped chives.

CHERRY CHOCOLATE SALAD

Makes 6 servings

1 pkg. non-instant vanilla
  pudding mix
1 pkg. cherry flavored
  gelatin
¾ C. water
1 (16 oz.) can tart red
  cherries in water

¾ C. frozen whipped
  topping, thawed
9 (2½″) chocolate
  graham crackers
½ C. miniature
  marshmallows

In medium saucepan over medium heat, combine dry vanilla pudding mix, dry cherry gelatin mix and water. Mix well and stir in cherries in juice. Heat, stirring often, until mixture thickens and begins to boil, being sure not to crush the cherries. Spoon mixture into a large bowl and place bowl on wire rack. Let stand for 45 minutes. Stir in whipped topping and place in refrigerator for 10 minutes. Break chocolate graham crackers into large pieces. Just before serving, stir in graham cracker pieces and miniature marshmallows.

COCOA CHICKEN SALAD
Makes 6 servings

2 T. ground cumin
2 T. curry powder
1 tsp. salt
1 tsp. pepper
1½ T. cocoa powder
6 boneless, skinless chicken breasts
1 T. vegetable oil
¾ C. olive oil

¼ C. apple cider vinegar
8 C. salad greens
1 large red bell pepper, cut into strips
1 large orange bell pepper, cut into strips
1 pt. cherry tomatoes, cut in half
1 medium cucumber, sliced
12 radishes, sliced

Preheat oven to 350° and lightly grease a baking sheet. In a small bowl, combine ground cumin, curry powder, salt, pepper and cocoa powder and mix well. Rub chicken breasts with vegetable oil and sprinkle 1 heaping teaspoon cocoa mixture over each chicken breast and rub mixture over entire chicken surface. Set aside remaining cocoa mixture. Place coated chicken on prepared baking sheet.

Bake in oven for 20 to 25 minutes, or until juices are clear. Remove from oven and let cool before slicing chicken into strips. In a medium bowl, combine remaining cocoa mixture, olive oil and apple cider vinegar. Cover and chill in refrigerator. To serve, divide salad greens evenly onto 6 plates. Arrange cooked chicken slices, red and orange bell pepper strips, tomatoes, cucumbers and radishes. Serve immediately with chilled dressing.

"Other things are just food.

But chocolate's chocolate."

Patrick Skene Catling

CARAMEL-NUT COCOA SALAD

Makes 10 to 12 servings

1 (5 oz.) pkg. instant vanilla
   pudding mix
1 C. milk
1 (12 oz.) container frozen
   whipped topping, thawed
6 apples, peeled, cored
   and chopped

6 bars chocolate candy
   with peanuts, broken
¼ C. seedless grapes,
   optional

Prepare pudding according to package directions, using the 1 cup milk. Blend in whipped topping until smooth. Mix in chopped apples, candy bar pieces and seedless grapes. Toss mixture until well incorporated and chill in refrigerator until ready to serve.

FRUIT COCOA SALAD TOSS

Makes 4 servings

3 slices chewy European
   bread
2 ripe bananas, chilled
2 ripe kiwis, chilled

2 ripe nectarines, chilled
Juice of ½ lemon
2 tsp. cocoa powder

Cut the European bread slices into cubes and place in a serving bowl. Cut the bananas, kiwis and nectarines into small cubes and place in serving bowl. Squeeze juice from lemon half over bread cubes and cubed fruit. Using a sifter, sift cocoa powder over bread and fruit and toss until evenly coated. Serve immediately.

RAINBOW COVERED APPLES
Makes 6 apples

6 medium sweet-tart apples
Popsicle sticks
1 lb. semi-sweet chocolate,
  cut into chunks

1 C. M&Ms or other
toppings

Twist off apple stems and push one Popsicle stick down into core of each apple, being careful not to push all the way through the apple. Place apples in refrigerator while preparing chocolate coating. In a double boiler over high heat, slowly melt chocolate, stirring occasionally until melted and smooth. Remove from heat and stir until mixture is warm, but not hot. Dunk each chilled apple into the chocolate, allowing excess chocolate to drip back into bowl. Roll the apples in the chocolate until coated all the way up to the stick, using a spoon to help coat apples. Place M&Ms in a single layer on a baking sheet. Roll apples over M&Ms until coated. Set the coated apples on a separate baking sheet lined with waxed paper. Place apples in refrigerator until the chocolate has set.

CHOCOLATE SOUP

Makes 4 servings

½ C. plus 1 T. sugar
5 T. flour
2 T. cocoa powder
4 C. milk

½ tsp. vanilla
Salt to taste
3 slices bread
¼ C. butter

Preheat broiler. In a medium oven-safe bowl, combine sugar, flour and cocoa powder. Place mixture under broiler for 1 to 2 minutes, stirring frequently, until browned. Add about 2 tablespoons milk and stir until mixture is creamy. Place remaining milk in a medium saucepan and bring to a boil. Slowly stir in cocoa mixture and return to a boil. Reduce heat and mix in vanilla and salt to taste. Remove from heat and keep warm. In a medium saucepan over medium heat, melt butter. Cut bread slices into cubes and heat in saucepan, turning until golden brown on all sides. Ladle soup mixture into bowls and mix some of the toasted bread cubes into each serving. Serve immediately.

CHILI CON COCOA
Makes 14 servings

¼ C. vegetable oil
1½ C. chopped onion
2 lbs. ground beef or turkey
2 T. cocoa powder
2 T. chili powder
2 tsp. cayenne pepper
1 tsp. salt
½ tsp. allspice
½ tsp. cinnamon

7 C. whole tomatoes in juice
1⅓ C. tomato paste
1 C. water
½ C. shaved milk chocolate
3 C. dark red kidney
  beans in liquid
14 (8 oz.) miniature bread
  bowls, hollowed

In a large saucepan over medium heat, heat vegetable oil. Stir in chopped onion and sauté for 3 minutes, or until onion is tender. Mix in ground beef or turkey and heat until meat is browned. Drain oil from saucepan and stir in cocoa powder, chili powder, cayenne pepper, salt, allspice, cinnamon, tomatoes and juice, tomato paste and water. Bring mixture to a boil and reduce heat. Stir in shaved milk chocolate and beans in liquid. Reduce heat and let simmer for 30 minutes. Ladle about 1 cup chili into each hollowed bread bowl.

"Chocolate flows in deep dark, sweet waves, a river to ignite my mind and alert my senses."

Author Unknown

CHOCOLATE CHIP CHEESE BALL
Makes 32 servings

1 (8 oz.) pkg. cream
  cheese, softened
½ C. butter, softened
¾ C. powdered sugar
2 T. brown sugar

¼ tsp. vanilla
¾ C. miniature
  chocolate chips
¾ C. finely chopped
  pecans

In a medium mixing bowl, beat together cream cheese and butter until smooth. Mix in powdered sugar, brown sugar and vanilla. Stir in chocolate chips. Cover with plastic wrap and chill in the refrigerator for 2 hours. Shape chilled cream cheese mixture into a ball and wrap in plastic wrap. Chill in refrigerator at least 1 hour. Before serving, roll cheese ball in finely chopped pecans. Serve with various crackers.

CARAMEL COCOA PARTY MIX

Makes 8 servings

2 C. crispy corn cereal
squares
2 C. small pretzel twists
1 C. dry roasted peanuts

20 caramels, unwrapped
1 (11½ oz.) pkg. milk
chocolate chips

Coat a 9 x 13″ baking dish with nonstick cooking spray. In a large bowl, combine cereal, pretzels and peanuts. In a medium microwave-safe bowl, place caramels and milk chocolate chips. Heat chocolate and caramels in microwave for 1 minute, remove and stir. Return to microwave for 20 second intervals, stirring after each heating, until mixture is smooth. Pour melted chocolate mixture over cereal mixture and toss gently, but quickly, until coated. Spread mixture evenly into prepared baking dish. Let cool for 30 to 45 minutes, or until firm. To serve, break into bite size pieces.

SNOW COVERED SNACKERS
Makes 9 cups

9 C. corn cereal squares
1 (6 oz.) pkg. chocolate chips
½ C. peanut butter

¼ C. margarine or butter
1 tsp. vanilla
1½ C. powdered sugar

In a large bowl, place corn cereal squares and set aside. In a medium microwave-safe bowl, place chocolate chips, peanut butter and margarine. Heat in microwave for 1 minute, remove and stir. Return to microwave for 30 seconds, or until mixture is completely melted and smooth when stirred. Remove from microwave and mix in vanilla. Pour chocolate mixture over cereal in bowl, stirring and tossing until evenly coated. Pour coated cereal into large ziplock bag. Add powdered sugar to bag and seal. Shake bag until chocolate covered cereal is coated in powdered sugar. Spread mixture onto waxed paper to cool. Store in an airtight container in refrigerator.

EASY CORNFLAKE CAKES

Makes 1½ dozen

1 (2 oz.) bar semi-sweet   2½ C. cornflakes
  or milk chocolate

In a double boiler over boiling water, place chocolate bar. Heat chocolate, stirring until melted. In the meantime, line 18 muffin cups with paper liners. Mix cornflakes into melted chocolate, stirring gently, until cereal is completely coated in chocolate. Once cereal is coated in chocolate, place about 1 tablespoon of the cereal mixture into each paper liner and let set until hardened.

SMARTIE CHOCOLATE SQUARES

Makes 16 squares

½ C. butter
½ C. brown sugar
1 egg, beaten
1 C. shredded coconut
¾ C. flour

2 T. cocoa powder
1 tsp baking powder
1 C. milk chocolate chips
2 small packets
Smarties candy

Preheat oven to 350°. Line a jellyroll pan with waxed paper. In a saucepan over low heat, melt butter. Stir in brown sugar and mix until smooth. Remove from heat and cool for 5 minutes. Stir in the egg and coconut. Into a medium bowl, sift flour, cocoa powder and baking powder. Toss flour mixture together and slowly stir flour mixture into brown sugar mixture, mixing until well combined. Turn mixture out into prepared pan and, using a spatula, spread mixture into an even layer. Bake in oven for 15 to 17 minutes, or until mixture is just firm when touched in the center. Remove from the oven and sprinkle with milk chocolate chips. Sprinkle Smarties candy over the chocolate and press down lightly. Return pan to the oven for an additional 5 minutes. Remove from oven and let cool.

THE ORIGINAL
NO-BAKE COOKIE
Makes 2 dozen

2 C. sugar
¼ lb. butter
½ C. milk
3 T. cocoa powder

1 tsp. vanilla
½ C. creamy peanut butter
3 C. quick cooking oats

In a large saucepan over medium heat, combine sugar, butter, milk and cocoa powder. Bring mixture to a boil for one minute. Remove from the heat and mix in the vanilla and creamy peanut butter. Toss all together until well combined and stir in quick cooking oats. Mix together until oats are well incorporated. Drop mixture by tablespoonfuls onto waxed paper. Place cookies in refrigerator until hardened, about 1 hour. Store leftovers in refrigerator.

SIMPLE CHOCOLATE SOUFFLE

Makes 4 or 6 servings

6 T. butter
4 (1 oz.) bars semi-sweet
  chocolate, grated
¼ C. sugar

1¾ T. cornstarch
2 eggs
2 egg yolks

In a small saucepan over low heat, combine butter and grated chocolate. Heat, stirring frequently, until melted and set aside. In a medium bowl, combine sugar and cornstarch. In a separate bowl, using a wire whisk, beat together eggs and egg yolks. Stir melted chocolate mixture into the sugar mixture and, using a wire whisk, mix until well combined. Add eggs and whisk just until smooth. Place in refrigerator overnight. Preheat oven to 400°. Line four 2″ to 3″ metal rings or soufflé dishes, or six smaller round dishes, with greased parchment paper. Line a baking sheet with parchment paper and set the molds on the sheet. Fill molds ²/₃ full with chilled mixture, making sure they do no leak. Place filled molds on top rack in oven. Bake for 20 minutes and remove baking sheet from oven. Place soufflé dishes on plates and serve. If using molds, carefully slide each mold onto a metal spatula and place on serving plate. Lift off mold and remove parchment paper.

"Exercise is a dirty word...

Every time I say it, I wash

my mouth out with chocolate."

Author Unknown

"*Chocolate causes certain endocrine glands to secrete hormones that affect your feelings and behavior by making you happy. Therefore, it counteracts depression, in turn reducing the stress of depression. Your stress-free life helps you maintain a youthful disposition, both physically and mentally. So, eat lots of chocolate!*"

Elaine Sherman

STORING CHOCOLATE

One of the great advantages for chocolate lovers is that chocolate keeps very well. Chocolate has, for centuries, been used by travelers, adventurers and armies because of its high energy content and the fact that it does not spoil very easily.

The biggest problem that can arise during the storage of chocolate is the separation of the cocoa butter or sugar from the rest of the mixture. This separation causes a discoloration on the surface of the chocolate from the melting and recrystallizing that could occur in either extreme cold or hot temperatures. This result is not dangerous, but can affect the taste and appearance.

Chocolate should never be stored in the refrigerator for significant periods of time, as condensation and separation will cause a degradation of the flavor. Optimal storage for chocolate is well wrapped and placed in a cold, dark, dry, well-ventilated area.

DREAMY CHOCOLATE CAKE
Makes 12 servings

1 (18¼ oz.) pkg. devils
  food cake mix
1 C. sour cream
1 C. water
⅓ C. vegetable oil
3 large eggs
7 (1 oz.) squares bittersweet
  chocolate, chopped
3 C. heavy whipping
  cream, divided

5 T. light corn syrup, divided
1 T. vanilla
4 large egg yolks
5 T. instant vanilla
  pudding mix
4 (1 oz.) squares semi-
  sweet chocolate, chopped
2 (1 oz.) squares dark
  chocolate, chopped
1 T. butter, softened

Preheat oven to 350°. Lightly grease and flour two 9″ round cake pans. In a large mixing bowl, combine devils food cake mix, sour cream, water, vegetable oil and eggs. Beat at high speed for 2 minutes, scraping sides of bowl while mixing. Pour mixture into prepared cake pans. Bake in oven for 25 to 35 minutes, or until a toothpick inserted in center of cake comes out clean. Remove cakes from oven and let cool for 15 minutes. To prepare frosting, in a microwave-safe bowl, place chopped bittersweet chocolate. Heat in microwave at 30 second intervals until melted and smooth. Set chocolate aside to cool. In a small saucepan over medium low heat, combine ½ cup heavy whipping cream, 4 tablespoons corn syrup, vanilla and egg yolks. Heat, whisking constantly, for 5 to 6 minutes, or until mixture has reached 160° at coats the back of a spoon. Pour yolk mixture through a fine sieve into chocolate. Whisk briskly, until chocolate is shiny and satin-smooth. Let mixture cool to about 80°. In a large mixing bowl, beat 2 cups heavy cream and vanilla pudding mix at medium high speed until stiff peaks form. Fold cooled chocolate mixture into whipped cream. To assemble cake, place 1 cake layer on serving platter and frost generously with frosting. Top with second cake layer and spread remaining frosting over top and sides of cake. Refrigerate for 1 hour. Meanwhile, in a small saucepan over medium heat, combine remaining ½ cup heavy cream and remaining 1 tablespoon corn syrup. Bring mixture to a simmer and remove from heat. Mix in chopped semi-sweet chocolate and chopped dark chocolate. Let stand for 5 minutes before stirring until smooth. Mix in butter, stirring until melted. Let stand until mixture is lukewarm but still pourable, about 20 minutes. Drizzle mixture over cake and return to refrigerator until ready to serve.

SWIRLED CHOCOLATE SWEET POTATO CHEESECAKE
Makes 10 to 12 servings

1¾ C. graham cracker
  crumbs
¼ C. sugar
¼ C. butter, melted
4 (8 oz.) pkgs. cream
  cheese, softened
1 C. brown sugar

1 (15 oz.) can sweet
  potatoes or yams in
  light syrup, drained
3 eggs
1 T. vanilla
1 tsp. pumpkin pie spice
2 C. milk chocolate chips

Preheat oven to 350°. In a medium bowl, combine graham cracker crumbs, sugar and melted butter, stirring until well blended. Press mixture firmly and evenly into bottom and 1 ½″ up sides of a 9″ springform pan. In a large mixing bowl, beat together softened cream cheese and brown sugar at medium high speed until fluffy. In a separate bowl, using a fork, mash drained sweet potatoes. Stir mashed sweet potatoes into cream cheese mixture and continue to beat until smooth, about 2 minutes. Add eggs, one at a time, beating at low speed after each addition. Mix in vanilla and pumpkin pie spice and beat at low speed for 1 additional minute, scraping sides of bowl as needed. In a medium microwave-safe bowl, place milk chocolate chips. Heat in microwave for 1 minute, remove and stir. If necessary, return to microwave for 15 second intervals, stirring after each heating, until chocolate is melted when stirred. Stir ¾ cup of the cream cheese mixture into melted chocolate, mixing until smooth. Spoon half of the cream cheese mixture into prepared crust. Spoon half of the chocolate mixture over top and swirl layers together using a knife. Top with remaining cream cheese mixture followed by remaining chocolate mixture and swirl again to outer edges of pan. Bake for 1 hour and 15 minutes, or until center is just set. Remove from oven and let cool on a wire rack. Chill in refrigerator until ready to serve. Store leftovers in refrigerator.

PEANUT BUTTER CUPS

Makes 12 candies

9 (1 oz.) bars bittersweet
chocolate, chopped,
divided
1 C. peanut butter

½ C. powdered sugar
Pinch of salt
12 to 15 banana chips

Cut the top half off of each 12 paper liner cups. In a medium microwave-safe bowl, place ¾ of the chopped bittersweet chocolate. Heat in microwave for 1 minute, remove and stir. Continue to microwave for 20 second intervals until chocolate is melted and smooth when stirred. Set aside for 2 to 3 minutes and stir in remaining ¼ of the chopped chocolate, mixing until all is melted and smooth. Fill each prepared paper liner with 1 teaspoonful of the melted chocolate. Using the back of a spoon, or a clean paintbrush, spread melted chocolate up inner sides of one paper liner until completely covered. Place chocolate coated liner in a muffin tin and repeat with the remaining muffin cups. Place muffin tin in refrigerator until chocolate hardens. In a medium bowl, combine peanut butter, pow-

dered sugar and salt, mixing until well combined. Spoon mixture into a large ziplock bag and seal. When chocolate in paper liners has hardened, remove from refrigerator. Place peanut butter mixture in ziplock bag in microwave and heat for 45 seconds. Remove from microwave and cut one of the bottom corners off of the plastic bag. Pipe peanut butter filling into each chocolate cup. Place 1 banana chip over each cup and return muffin tin to refrigerator until peanut butter filling has hardened, about 15 to 20 minutes. Remove paper liners before serving.

THIN MINTS
Makes 32 mints

1 (12 oz.) pkg. chocolate
chips
1 (6 oz.) pkg. white
chocolate chips

2 to 3 drops peppermint oil
3 to 4 drops green
food coloring

Line an 8″ square baking dish with aluminum foil, allowing foil to hang up over sides of baking dish. In a double boiler over barely simmering water, heat chocolate
chips until half the chips are melted. Remove from heat
and stir until chocolate is completely melted and smooth.
Spread half of the semi-sweet chocolate evenly in bottom
of prepared pan and place pan in refrigerator for 5 to 10
minutes. Meanwhile, heat white chocolate chips in same
manner, until half the chips are melted. Remove from heat
and stir until completely melted and smooth. Mix in peppermint oil and food coloring until blended and light green
in color. Spread melted chocolate in an even layer over
cooled chocolate layer in pan. Return to refrigerator for 10
minutes, or until firm. If necessary, reheat remaining half of

melted chocolate and spread over mint chocolate layer. Return to refrigerator until solid. To serve, lift chocolate layers from baking dish and transfer to a cutting board. Peel away aluminum foil and cut chocolate into sixteen 2″ squares, then cut each square into a triangle.

"And above all...

think chocolate!"

Betty Crocker

CHOCOLATE MARQUISE
Makes 8 to 10 servings

8 (1 oz.) squares bittersweet chocolate, coarsely chopped	4 large eggs
	¼ C. sugar
	¼ C. water
8 T. butter, cut into pieces	Whipped topping

Place a medium heat-proof bowl inside a large skillet. Fill skillet with about 1˝ water and bring water to a simmer. Place coarsely chopped chocolate and butter pieces in bowl, stirring frequently, until chocolate is almost melted. Remove bowl from heat and stir until chocolate and butter are completely melted and smooth. Set aside. In a medium metal bowl, using a wire whisk, combine eggs and sugar, whisking until well blended. Stir in water and place metal bowl in same skillet of barely simmer water. Stir constantly to prevent eggs from scrambling, heat until mixture reaches 160° on a candy thermometer.

Remove metal bowl with egg mixture from skillet and, using an electric mixer, beat eggs at high speed for 3 to 4 minutes, or until soft peaks form. Fold ¼ of the egg mixture into the melted chocolate. Fold in half of the remaining egg mixture, stirring until nearly blended. Add remaining ¼ of the egg mixture and fold gently until evenly incorporated. Immediately divide mousse mixture evenly into 8 to 10 small ramekins, or use as a filling for cake or other dessert. Chill in refrigerator at least 1 hour before serving. If desired, serve with whipped topping.

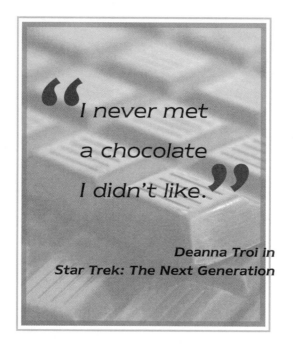

"*I never met a chocolate I didn't like.*"

Deanna Troi in
Star Trek: The Next Generation

CHOCOLATE SCOTCHEROOS

Makes 4 dozen bars

1 C. sugar	6 C. crispy rice cereal
1 C. light corn syrup	1 C. chocolate chips
1 C. peanut butter	1 C. butterscotch chips

Coat a 9 x 13″ baking dish with non-stick cooking spray and set aside. In a medium saucepan over medium heat, combine sugar and corn syrup. Bring mixture to a boil, stirring occasionally. Remove from heat and add peanut butter, mixing until smooth. Place crispy rice cereal in a large bowl and pour peanut butter mixture over cereal, tossing until well incorporated. Press coated cereal in an even layer into prepared pan. In a double boiler over simmering water, place chocolate chips and butterscotch chips, stirring frequently, until melted and smooth. Remove from heat and spread melted chocolate mixture evenly over cereal layer. Chill in refrigerator until chocolate has hardened. To serve, cut into 1 x 2″ bars.

THE TRUTH ABOUT CHOCOLATE

CHOCOLATE AND ACNE

In the past, the rumor that chocolate causes acne led to hundreds of teenagers and people with sensitive skin to turn their nose up at the delicious sweet. However, over the past two decades, research conducted at the Department of Dermatology at the University of Pennsylvania School of Medicine and elsewhere, has revealed that chocolate neither causes nor aggravates acne. In fact, the studies revealed that acne cannot be primarily linked to a person's diet at all.

CHOCOLATE AND CAFFEINE

Soon, another rumor spread accusing chocolate of containing large amounts of caffeine. In fact, eating chocolate later in the day was, at one time, thought to be detrimental to a good night's sleep. In reality, the amount of caffeine ingested in a normal quantity of chocolate is very small, making the role of caffeine in chocolate a non-issue. For example, 1.4 ounces of milk chocolate contains only six milligrams of caffeine, which is about the same amount found in a cup of decaffeinated coffee.

IS CHOCOLATE GOOD FOR YOU?

Willing it to be true, chocoholics have always proclaimed, "Yes, chocolate is good for you!" According to recent studies, chocolate-lovers can revel in their statement, as chocolate actually provides a number of nutrients that the body requires daily.

A 1.4 ounce chocolate bar contains about three grams of protein, 15 percent of the Daily Recommended Value of riboflavin, nine percent of the Daily Recommended Value of calcium and seven percent of the Daily Recommended Value for iron. Throw in some almonds or peanuts and the nutrients increase. Now, if it just weren't for those pesky calories, sugars and fats.

HUGS N' KISSES TORTE
Makes 8 servings

1 (8 oz.) pkg. Hershey's
  kisses, unwrapped
½ C. plus ⅓ C. heavy
  whipping cream, divided
2 tsp. butter, softened
½ tsp. vanilla

1 (10¾ oz.) loaf frozen
  pound cake,
  partially thawed
10 Hershey's Hugs,
  unwrapped

In a medium saucepan over low heat, place unwrapped Hershey's kisses and ⅓ cup heavy whipping cream. Cook, stirring frequently, until chocolate is melted and smooth. Remove from heat and stir in butter and vanilla, mixing until butter has completely melted. Transfer mixture to a medium bowl and place in refrigerator until mixture is firm enough to spread, about 1 hour. Meanwhile, slice thawed pound cake horizontally into 3 even layers. Place bottom layer on serving plate and top with ⅓ of the chocolate filling, spreading evenly. Top with second cake layer and spread another ⅓ of the filling over cake layer. Place remaining cake layer on top. In a medium mixing bowl, beat remaining ½ cup heavy cream at medium high speed until stiff peaks form. Fold in remaining chocolate mixture, mixing gently until well incorporated. Spread mixture over top and sides of cake and place in refrigerator about 6 hours. Garnish top of torte with Hershey's Hugs chocolate before serving.

"All I really need is love,

but a little chocolate now

and then doesn't hurt!"

Lucy Van Pelt in Peanuts comic strip

GERMAN CHOCOLATE CHEESECAKE

Makes 9 servings

1 C. graham cracker crumbs

6 T. butter, melted

¼ C. plus ⅔ C. sugar, divided

¼ C. finely chopped pecans

¼ C. shredded coconut

4 T. cocoa powder, divided

2 C. heavy whipping cream, divided

8 (1 oz.) bars semi-sweet chocolate, grated

1 (6 oz.) pkg. cream cheese, softened

4 eggs

2 tsp. vanilla, divided

½ C. sour cream

2 T. powdered sugar

Preheat oven to 325°. In a medium bowl, combine graham cracker crumbs, melted butter, ¼ cup sugar, finely chopped pecans, shredded coconut and 2 tablespoon cocoa powder. Mix until well incorporated. Press mixture into bottom and half way up sides of a 9˝ springform pan. Bake in oven for 10 minutes. Remove from oven and let cool.

Meanwhile, in a small saucepan over low heat, combine 1 cup heavy whipping cream and grated chocolate. Heat, stirring frequently, until chocolate is completely melted. Remove from heat and let cool slightly. In a medium mixing bowl, beat cream cheese and remaining $2/3$ cup sugar at medium speed until lightened and fluffy. Add eggs, one at a time, beating well after each addition. Stir in melted chocolate mixture, 1 teaspoon vanilla and sour cream. Pour mixture into baked crust. Return to oven for 65 to 70 minutes, or until outer 2″ of cake are firm and center is slightly soft. Remove from oven and let cool before chilling in refrigerator for several hours or overnight. To prepare topping, in a deep mixing bowl, combine remaining 2 tablespoon cocoa powder, remaining 1 cup heavy cream, powdered sugar and remaining 1 teaspoon vanilla. Chill mixture in refrigerator for 20 minutes. Remove from refrigerator and beat at high speed until stiff peaks form. Place cake on serving platter and remove springform pan. Serve cheesecake with dollops of whipped chocolate cream.

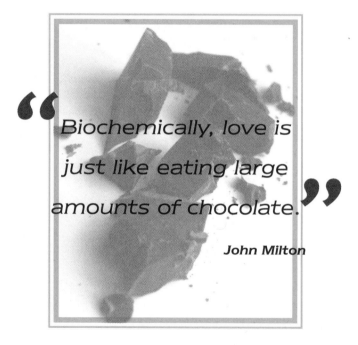

"Biochemically, love is just like eating large amounts of chocolate.

John Milton

SOFT COCOA CARAMELS

Makes 64 caramels

1 C. sugar
½ C. light corn syrup
1 C. heavy whipping cream,
   room temperature

2 (1 oz.) squares
   bittersweet chocolate,
   finely chopped
1 T. butter

In a heavy saucepan over medium heat, combine sugar and corn syrup, mixing until sugar is completely moistened. Bring the mixture to a boil and heat, without stirring, until mixture turns a very light caramel color, about 5 minutes. Remove from the heat and, very slowly, pour heavy whipping cream into hot sugar mixture, being careful, as mixture will bubble. Stir until well combined. Return mixture to stovetop over medium low heat and bring to a simmer, stirring occasionally, until mixture registers 238° on a candy thermometer, about 12 to 15 minutes. Remove from the heat and whisk in finely chopped chocolate and butter, mixing until smooth. Pour the mixture into a greased 8″ square baking dish. Let mixture cool for 2 hours before cutting into 1″ squares.

YUMMY MUD PIE
Makes 9 to 10 servings

10 T. butter, divided

2 C. finely ground Oreo cookies

½ C. chopped cashews

1½ pkgs. (17 oz.) chocolate chips, divided

5 large eggs, separated

⅔ C. malt powder

¼ C. plus 2½ T. sugar, divided

1 (1 oz.) bar unsweetened chocolate, grated

1¼ C. heavy whipping cream

6 egg whites

¼ C. sugar

In a small microwave-safe bowl, melt 2 tablespoons butter. In a large bowl, combine ground Oreos, chopped cashews and melted butter. Toss until well combined and press the mixture into the bottom of a 10″ springform pan. Place in refrigerator. In a double boiler over simmering water, place 12 ounces chocolate chips and remaining 8 tablespoons butter. Heat, stirring frequently, until mixture is melted and smooth. Remove from heat and let cool slightly. Using a wire whisk, whisk in 5 egg yolks and malt powder. Meanwhile, in a medium mixing bowl, beat 5 egg whites at medium high speed until soft peaks form. Slowly mix in 2½ tablespoons sugar until whipped mixture is stiff and glossy. Fold in melted chocolate mixture. Pour over layer in springform pan and spread evenly with a rubber spatula. Return to refrigerator. Meanwhile, in a double boiler over simmering water, place remaining 5 ounces chocolate chips and grated unsweetened chocolate. Mix until chocolate is completely melted and smooth. Remove from heat and let cool slightly. In a large mixing bowl, beat heavy cream at medium high speed until soft peaks form and chill in refrigerator. In a separate mixing bowl, beat an additional 6 egg whites at medium high speed until soft peaks form. Slowly beat in remaining ¼ cup sugar. Fold egg whites mixture into chocolate mixture, adding ⅓ at a time. Fold whipped cream into chocolate mixture. Pour mixture over layers in springform pan and return to refrigerator. Chill at least 3 hours or overnight. To serve, place springform pan on a serving platter and slowly remove the sides of the pan.

CHOCOLATE BANANA PIE

Makes 9 servings

1 (9″) prepared pie crust dough

3 T. cornstarch, divided

½ C. plus 2 T. sugar, divided

2 T. cocoa powder

½ teaspoons salt

1⅓ C. milk, divided

1 oz. chocolate chips

2 large eggs

1 T. butter

2 tsp. vanilla

2 oz. Neufchatel cheese, or cream cheese

2 C. sliced bananas

1½ C. whipped topping

Preheat oven to 400°. Bake prepared pie crust layer in a 9″ pie pan until browned, about 14 minutes. Remove from oven and let cool for 10 minutes. In a small saucepan over low heat, combine 1 tablespoon cornstarch, 2 tablespoons sugar, cocoa powder and ¼ teaspoon salt. Gradually whisk in ⅓ cup milk. Increase heat to medium low and cook for 2 minutes. Stir in chocolate chips. Bring mixture to a boil, stirring constantly, until slightly thickened. Remove from heat and spread chocolate mixture over baked pie crust, spreading evenly with the back of a spoon. In a medium saucepan over medium heat, combine remaining 2 table-spoons cornstarch, remaining 1 cup milk, remaining ½ cup sugar, remaining ¼ teaspoon salt, eggs and butter, stirring constantly with a wire whisk. Bring mixture to a boil, reduce heat to low and continue to cook for 2 minutes. Remove from heat and stir in vanilla. In a medium mixing bowl, beat Neufchatel cheese at low speed for 30 seconds. Add ⅓ cup egg mixture to Neufchatel cheese and beat until just blended. Stir in remaining egg mixture. Arrange banana slices over chocolate layer in pie crust. Spoon filling mixture over banana slices. Cover with plastic wrap, letting plastic rest on surface of custard. Chill in refrigerator at least 4 hours. Remove plastic wrap and spread whipped topping over custard before serving.

BLIZZARD ICE CREAM CAKE

Makes 12 servings

1 gallon vanilla ice cream
1 (20 oz.) pkg. Oreo cookies

1 (12 oz.) container frozen
whipped topping, thawed

Soften ice cream in refrigerator. Place Oreos in a large Zip-loc bag and seal. Crush Oreos by rolling over sealed bag with a rolling pin. In a large bowl, mix softened vanilla ice cream and crushed Oreo cookies until well combined. Fold in whipped topping, mixing until well incorporated. Transfer mixture to a 9 x 13″ glass baking dish and spread in an evenly layer. Place in freezer for 2 hours before serving.

FLAKEY CHOCOLATE FINGERS

1 (8 oz.) pkg. puff pastry dough
1 (4 oz.) pkg. cream cheese

2 T. yogurt
4 oz. chocolate chips
1 (8 oz.) pkg. fresh raspberries

Divide puff pastry into three parts. Roll out each part on a lightly floured flat surface into 4 x 12″ pieces. Put pastry strips on a greased baking sheet and prick with a fork. Place in refrigerator for 30 minutes. Preheat oven to 425°. Bake pastry strips until golden brown, about 15 minutes and let cool. Meanwhile, in a double boiler over simmering water, melt chocolate chips, stirring occasionally. In a bowl, beat cream cheese and yogurt at medium speed until well combined. Stir in half of the melted chocolate. Place one pastry strip on a cutting board and spread half of the cream cheese mixture over top. Top with another pastry strip and remaining half of the cream cheese mixture. Top with third pastry strip. Spread melted chocolate over top. Chill in refrigerator for 30 minutes. To serve, cut layers into 1″ fingers and garnish with fresh raspberries.

CHOCOLATE COVERED STRAWBERRIES
Makes 24 strawberries

24 fresh strawberries
with stems

16 oz. milk chocolate chips
2 T. shortening

Insert one toothpick into the top of each strawberry. In a double boiler over simmering water, place milk chocolate chips and shortening, stirring occasionally until melted and smooth. Holding strawberries by the toothpicks, dip each strawberry into the melted chocolate mixture, using a spoon to help fully coat the strawberries. Turn strawberries upside down and insert the toothpick into a piece of Styrofoam, allowing for the chocolate to cool. Remove toothpicks before serving.

INDEX

" In the end, Charlie Bucket won a chocolate factory. But Willy Wonka had something even better, a family. And one thing was absolutely certain – life had never been sweeter. "

From Charlie and the Chocolate Factory